HORRIBLE HABITATS
Caves and Crevices

Sharon Katz Cooper

Chicago, Illinois

www.heinemannraintree.com
Visit our website to find out more information about Heinemann-Raintree books.

To order:
☎ Phone 888-454-2279
💻 Visit www.heinemannraintree.com
to browse our catalog and order online.

© 2010 Raintree
an imprint of Capstone Global Library, LLC
Chicago, Illinois

Edited by Charlotte Guillain, Rebecca Rissman, and Sian Smith
Designed by Joanna Hinton-Malivoire
Picture research by Tracy Cummins and Heather Mauldin
Originated by Chroma Graphics (Overseas) Pte. Ltd
Printed and bound in China by Leo Paper Products

14 13 12 11 10
10 9 8 7 6 5 4 3 2 1

Library of Congress Cataloging-in-Publication Data
Katz Cooper, Sharon.
Caves and crevices / Sharon Katz Cooper.
p. cm. -- (Horrible habitats)
Includes bibliographical references and index.
ISBN 978-1-4109-3494-9 (hc)
ISBN 978-1-4109-3502-1 (pb)
1. Caves--Juvenile literature. 2. Cave animals--Juvenile literature. I. Title.
GB601.2.K38 2009
591.75'84--dc22
                                    2009002908

Acknowledgments
The author and publisher are grateful to the following for permission to reproduce copyright material: Alamy pp. **19** (© Wild Places/Chris Howes), **22** (© Peter Arnold, Inc.); Animals Animals/Earth Scenes p. **8** (© Efital Photography); Ardea pp. **20** (© Nick Gordon), **21** (© Adrian Warren), **25** (© Pascal Goetgheluck), **27** (Brian Bevan); Getty Images pp. **5** (© Owen Lexington), **9** (© Joseph Barrak); Minden p. **23** (© Michael Durham); National Geographic pp. **12** (© Carsten Peter), **12** (© Paul Zahl), **15** (© Stephen Sharnoff); Nature Picture Library pp. **6** (© Juan Manuel Borrero), **7** (© Phil Chapman); Photolibrary pp. **17** (© Emanuele Biggi), **18** (© Ivan Vdovin); Photo Researchers, Inc. pp. **16** (© Dante Fenolio), **24** (© Pascal Goetgheluck); Shutterstock pp. **10** (© Dariusz Majgier), **11** (© David William Taylor), **28** worm (© Odin M. Eidskrem), **28** fish (© Elena Schweitzer), **28** spider (© STILLFX), **28** box (Yellowj); Visuals Unlimited pp. **4** (© William Palmer), **14** (© Rob & Ann Simpson), **26** (Ken Lucas).

Cover photograph of a pair of roosting bats reproduced with permission of Minden Pictures (© Thomas Marent).

Some words are shown in bold, **like this.** You can find out what they mean by looking in the glossary.

Contents

What Is a Habitat?

A **habitat** is a place where plants and animals get the things they need to live. They need food, water, and shelter.

grotto salamander

cave

6

This isopod lives in caves.

Caves are **habitats**. They are often filled with water. A **crevice** is a crack in a rock wall. The rocks and crevices in caves give animals lots of places to hide. What do you think cave animals eat?

7

Cave food has to come from outside the cave. Flowing water brings in seeds, nuts, and small animals. Cave animals poo and lay eggs. Anything that dies in the cave becomes food for another animal.

vulture

vulture poo

Very Long Legs!

Daddy longlegs are common in caves. Like spiders, they have eight long legs. If one of the legs gets chopped off, it can twitch by itself for more than an hour!

FUN FACT

Daddy longlegs
are also called
harvestmen.

11

Stinging in The Dark

Scorpions are related to spiders. Some caves are full of them! They use **pincers** to catch insects. They inject insects with poison from the **stinger** on their tails.

stinger

pincer

FUN FACT

Animals eaten by other animals are called **prey.** Scorpions use little claws from their mouths to pull off pieces of their prey. How delicious!

Lots and Lots of Legs

Cave millipedes eat dead and rotting plant and animal parts. One type of millipede makes its own light! Scientists think millipedes use this light to scare away animals that might eat them.

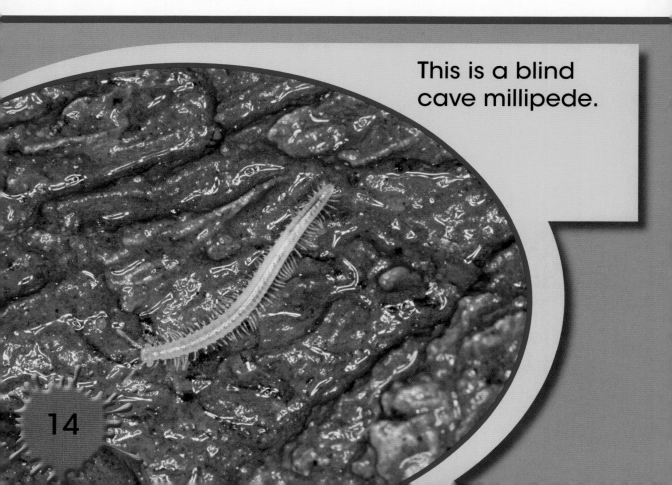

This is a blind cave millipede.

legs

15

Cave Giants

The giant salamander lives in caves in the United States and Asia. It can grow to be more than three feet long. That is about the same length as five soccer balls.

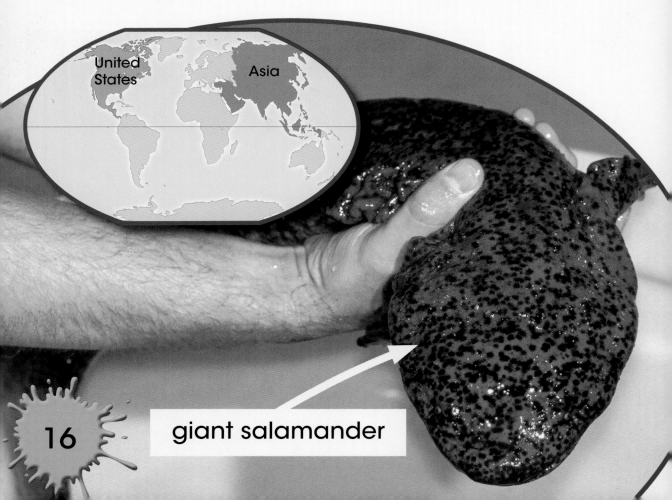

giant salamander

mouse

17

Here Come the Bats!

Some bats live in caves. They often live in large groups called **colonies**. They hang upside down and make lots of **guano**, or poo. This poo is food for many insects and other tiny animals in a cave.

These ticks are eating bat guano.

FUN FACT

Guano smells really, really bad!

Blood-Slurping Bats and Bugs

Vampire bats eat only blood. They fly out at night to look for cows, pigs, horses, or birds. They use their sharp teeth to cut a slit in an animal's leg. Then they slurp up the blood that drips out.

FUN FACT

Vampire bats are very small. They can lick up an animal's blood for a long time without waking it up!

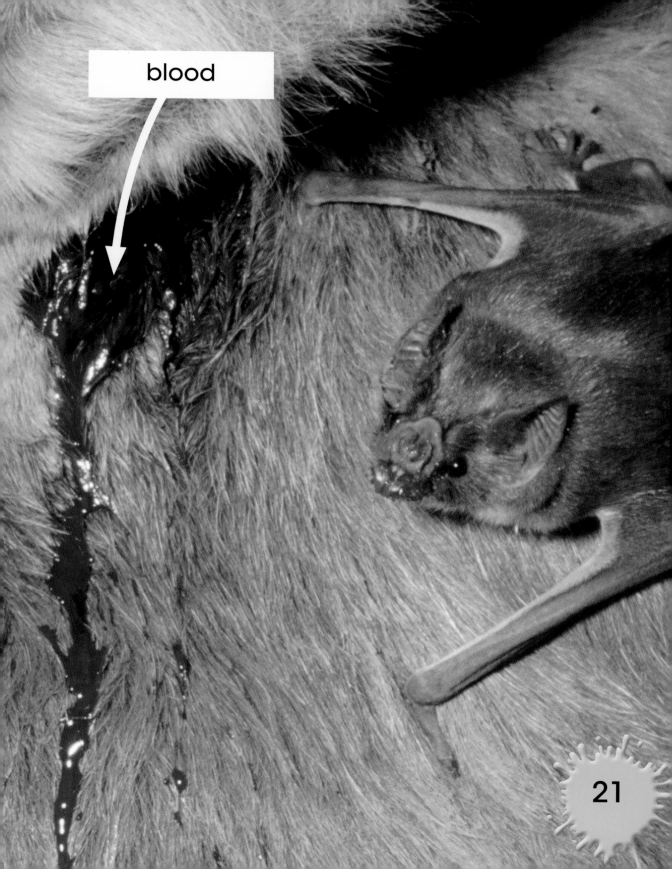

blood

21

bedbug

Bat bugs are tiny insects. They live off the blood of bats. They bite into a bat's skin and suck out blood. They bite other animals, too.

FUN FACT

Bat bugs are a lot like bedbugs. They will both bite people. Bat bugs sometimes even bite other bat bugs if they are filled with warm blood!

22

bat bug

Eating From the Inside Out

Gordian worms are **parasites** often found in cave animals. Parasites live off of other living animals. The worm's **larvae** or babies live inside other animals, such as crickets. The larva slowly eats the cricket's insides!

gordian worm

cricket

A gordian worm larva makes the cricket it lives in jump into water and drown. It does this so that the adult worm can come out and live in the water.

drowned cricket

gordian worm

No-Eyed Fish

The blind cavefish has no eyes and no sight. It has no need for eyes in a dark cave! It finds its way around by feeling movements in the water.

FUN FACT

The blind cavefish also has no color on its body.

Build Your Own Cave

What you need:
- an empty shoebox or cloth bag
- black paper
- tape
- a bunch of creepy cave "creatures" (such as modeling clay, a small hairbrush, a rubber spider, gummy worms, and a plastic fish)

What to do:

1. If you use a box, cut a hand-size hole in one of the short ends. Tape a piece of black paper over the hole to make a flap.

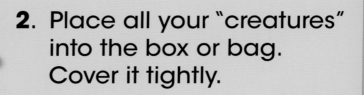

2. Place all your "creatures" into the box or bag. Cover it tightly.

3. Ask a friend to put their hand into the "cave." Ask the friend to try to identify each "creature" they touch.

4. How many can they get right? Is it hard to tell what things are without using your eyes?

Glossary

colonies large groups

crevices cracks in rock walls

guano bat or bird poo

habitat place where plants and animals live and grow

larvae baby insects

parasites animals that live off of other living animals

pincer claw that grips things and holds them tightly

prey animals eaten by other animals

stinger part of an animal used to attack and hurt or kill others

Find Out More

Find out

What is a megabat?

Books to Read

Galko, Francine. *Cave Animals.* Chicago: Heinemann Library, 2002.

Barnhill, Kelly Regan. *Animals with No Eyes: Cave Adaptations*. Mankato, MN: Capstone Press, 2008.

Websites

http://cavern.com/
This Website lets you search for caves near you!

http://www.colossalcave.com/cavetour.html
This Website takes you on a virtual tour of a cave.

http://www.kidzone.ws/animals/bats/facts.htm
Find out all about bats on this Website.

Index